D1006736

BOSTON COMMON PRESS
Brookline, Massachusetts

1996

Copyright © 1996 by The Editors of *Cook's Illustrated*

All rights reserved. No part of this book may be reproduced or transmitted in any manner whatsoever without written permission from the publisher, except in the case of brief quotations embodied in critical articles or reviews.

Boston Common Press
17 Station Street
Brookline, Massachusetts 02147

ISBN 0-936184-16-7
Library of Congress Cataloging-in Publication Data
The Editors of *Cook's Illustrated*
      How to make a pie: An illustrated step-by-step guide to the secrets of making the perfect pie/The Editors of *Cook's Illustrated* 1st ed.

      Includes 24 recipes and 40 illustrations.
      ISBN 0-936184-16-7 (hardback): $14.95
      I. Cooking.   I.Title
1996

Manufactured in the United States of America

Distributed by Boston Common Press, 17 Station Street, Brookline, MA 02147.

Cover and text design by Amy Klee

HOW TO MAKE A PIE

THE COOK'S ILLUSTRATED LIBRARY
No. 1

Illustrations by John Burgoyne

CONTENTS

introduction

IF THERE IS ONE ALL-AMERICAN DESSERT, it is the pie. There were pies on the Mayflower, and there have been pies wherever western European immigrants settled in the United States—which means everywhere. And for good reason. Dessert pies are a simple edible container filled with everything from fruit to custard to cream to sugar syrups. They keep well, are easy to transport, and usually taste better the next day.

In our small town in the Green Mountains of Vermont, I remember making dozens of pies with the local baker, Marie Briggs. In the early sixties we still baked with a wood stove, and my favorite pie, apple, was made from fruit gathered behind the house up by the old sugarhouse. I still favor our homegrown apples, Macoun and Northern Spy, for their bright, juicy taste. To this day, I maintain an orchard stocked with these two varieties, since they are not always easy to come across in the supermarket.

Today, however, pie making is becoming a lost art. Most modern home cooks have trouble with crusts, producing pastry that is often hard to roll out or tough when baked. In this book, we share with you the results of our extensive kitchen testing, which determined which ingredients are best suited to a tender, easy-to-make crust, which thickener does the best job with fruit pies, how to make a lemon meringue pie that doesn't weep, and how to produce a pumpkin pie with a crispy, not sodden, crust. You will also see, in forty hand-illustrated steps, the best techniques for working dough, edging pies, and solving common pie problems.

There are two ways you can use this book. You can use it as you would any recipe book. Find the recipe for Banana Cream Pie, for example, and you can make it right off the bat. But we also present a complete course in pie making here. If you take the time to work through it, preparing each of the major recipes and a few of the variations, you will become an expert pie maker, adept at a variety of crusts and fillings and the ways to combine them most effectively.

Let us know how you do. Like everyone else, we continue to learn, and your experiences add to the sum of our knowledge. Feel free to contact us at *Cook's Illustrated*, 17 Station Street, Brookline, MA 02147.

Christopher P. Kimball
Publisher and Editor
Cook's Illustrated

chapter one

THE BEST CRUSTS

AKING GOOD PIE CRUST CAN BE a simple procedure, but almost everyone who has tried can tell horror stories of crusts that turned out hard, soggy, flavorless, oversalted, underbaked, too crumbly, or unworkable. Advice is easy to come by: One expert says that butter is the secret to perfect crust; others swear by vegetable shortening, lard, even canola oil. Some omit salt, some omit sugar, some insist that working the dough by hand is essential, some use cake flour in addition to all-purpose flour, some freeze the dough, some do away with the rolling pin…and so on.

8

THE INGREDIENTS

Simple as it can be, the pie crust—essentially a combination of flour, water, and fat—raises numerous questions: What are the ideal proportions of the main ingredients? What else should be added for character? What methods should be used to combine these ingredients?

WHICH FAT IS BEST?

The most controversial ingredient in pastry is fat, so let's start with that. We've found that although all-butter crusts have good taste, they are not as flaky and fine-textured as those made with some shortening, which are our favorites. All-shortening crusts have great texture but lack flavor; oil-based crusts are flat and entirely unappealing; and those made with lard are not only heavy and strongly flavored but out of favor due to health issues. We've experimented with a variety of combinations and ultimately settled on a proportion of three parts butter to two parts shortening as optimal for both flavor and texture.

There's a reason shortening works: Vegetable shortenings such as Crisco are made from vegetable oil that has been hydrogenated in order to incorporate air and to raise its melting point above room temperature. (This is much the same process as "creaming" butter and sugar, in which the sharp sugar crystals cut into the fat and create pockets of air.) The absence of hydrogenation is why regular vegetable oils, which hold no more air than water, make poor pie doughs, whereas Crisco, which is about 10 percent gas, does a good job of lightening and tenderizing.

After much experimentation, we've settled on a ratio of flour to fat of about two parts to one. This ratio results in a relatively high-fat crust (you will find other recipes containing four parts of flour to one part of fat). But we found that the 2:1 proportion produces crusts that are easy to work and, when baked, are more tender and flavorful than any other.

FLOUR: ALL-PURPOSE OR CAKE?

The protein content of flour is important in any sort of baking. Bread flour, which is high in protein, produces strong, elastic dough. Low-protein pastry flour makes for a soft, tender crumb, the best for cakes. Pie crusts fall in between, and thus are best with all-purpose flour, a combination of bread and cake flours. No matter what we've tried—substituting cornstarch for part of the all-purpose flour (a cookie-baking trick that increases tenderness), adding a quarter teaspoon of baking powder to increase rise, and mixing cake flour with the all-purpose flour (again, to increase tenderness)—we've always come back to plain old all-purpose flour.

We've also tackled salt and sugar, which are much easier. After testing amounts ranging from a quarter teaspoon to as much as two tablespoons, we settled on one-half teaspoon of salt and one tablespoon of sugar, which greatly enhances flavor without shouting its presence.

STICK WITH WATER

We've also experimented with a variety of liquid ingredients, such as buttermilk, which has a dramatic impact on waffles, pancakes, and biscuits, and apple cider vinegar, an ingredient found in many old American cookbooks. No liquid additions have improved on our basic recipe. Stick with water.

THE TECHNIQUES

The techniques for making pie shells are straightforward and simple, and the food processor makes them easier than ever. What follows is a detailed description of the method (the Master Recipe for American Pie Dough follows this description); the same steps are illustrated for you on pages 22 through 43. Read through the description, then use the illustrations as a guide the first few times you make the shells—you probably won't need them after that.

MIXING THE DOUGH

You can make pie dough by hand, but the food processor, which is faster and easier, does a great job. In any case, first mix together the flour, sugar, and salt in a bowl. Cut the butter into cubes. Pulse the butter and flour together five times, then add the shortening and pulse four more times. Proper mixing is important: If you undermix, the crust will shrink when baked and became hard and crackly. If you overprocess, you'll get a crumbly, cookielike dough. (*See* figures 1 through 3.)

Using a pastry blender is also easy, especially if you grate very cold butter into the flour before adding the shortening and starting to mix. Then just push the pastry blender up and down in the dough, rolling it on its edge, until the mixture is the consistency of coarse meal. (*See* figures 4 and 5.)

Many people prefer to use their fingers: Grate the butter and then rub bits of it between your fingers, with the flour, for just a second at a time. Rub, then drop. Rub, drop. If the mixture starts to feel greasy, refrigerate it for a few minutes before continuing. (*See* figure 6.)

When you've combined the flour and fats, add the ice water. Use a rubber spatula and a folding motion to mix in the water, which exposes all of the dough to moisture without overworking it. This motion allows you to minimize the amount of water you use (the less water, the more tender the dough) and reduces the likelihood of overworking the dough. At this point, you should be able to press the dough into a ball with the spatula; add more water only if necessary. (*See* figures 7 and 8.)

ROLLING THE DOUGH

Once you have a ball of dough, flatten it into a disk, cover it with plastic wrap, and rest it in the refrigerator for thirty minutes. You can let the dough rest for longer (an hour is best if the weather is warm), but then let it warm up gradually to room temperature before attempting to roll it out, as long as forty-five minutes if the dough has rested overnight and the room is cool. (*See* figure 9.)

When you're ready to roll out the dough, flour a work surface very lightly; too much flour will be absorbed by the dough and cause it to toughen. Start with just a couple of tablespoons of flour and distribute it over the work surface using a flour sifter, a fine sieve, or your fingers; sprinkle the top of the dough with a little flour as well. Apply only light pressure to dough with a straight rolling pin and work from the center outwards to avoid rolling over the same area of dough more than necessary. If the dough becomes sticky and unworkable, put it back into the refrigerator for fifteen minutes instead of adding too much more flour (a bit more flour is okay). Every thirty to sixty seconds, turn the dough over with a dough scraper (a six-inch-long dull metal blade with a wooden handle) and rotate it a quarter of a turn. These steps make it easier to roll the dough to a uniform thickness and in a perfect circle, both of which ultimately minimize tearing and subsequent patching. Before rerolling, flour the work surface again, very lightly. (*See* figures 10 and 11.)

Roll the dough out so that its diameter is two inches more than that of the pie pan. The best way to make sure the circle of dough is big enough is to turn the pan over and place it on top of the dough; the dough should overlap by about an inch at every point. (*See* figure 12.)

▪▪ MOVING THE DOUGH

To get the dough into the pie pan, use your dough scraper to get under the dough and then gently roll it onto a rolling pin. With the dough draped over the pin, move the dough and unroll it into the pan. You can also fold the circle of dough in half and then in half again. Place the folded point of dough in the center of the pan and then unfold it gently. (*See* figures 13 and 14.)

For single-crust pies, push the dough firmly into the sides of the pie pan. This greatly reduces shrinkage, which can cause the dough to become so small it cannot hold enough filling. Trim the dough to one-half inch from the rim of the pan using scissors. Save some of the trimming scraps to patch tears or unevenly rolled parts of the dough (just brush the gap with a little water, then press in a bit of the reserved dough). Finally, fold the excess dough under itself, then finish with a design. (*See* figures 15 through 21.)

For a two-crust pie, don't trim the bottom shell first.

Instead, push it firmly into the sides of the pan, then fill the shell. Roll the remaining dough into a circle about one inch greater in diameter than the pan; it should overhang the bottom shell and pan by about one-half inch all around. Trim the edges of both shells together, then press them together and turn them under so that they are flush with the rim of the pan. Finish the shells with a design, then use a sharp knife to cut vents in the top shell. (*See* figures 22 through 24.)

PREBAKING PIE CRUSTS

For many pies it makes more sense to bake the crust, fully or partly, before filling it. There are several reasons for doing this. The most obvious is that there are times when the filling itself is not baked at all and thus needs to be poured into an already baked crust. But even when subsequent baking of the filling does occur, prebaking the shell promotes crispness and prevents liquid filling from soaking into a dough that would otherwise be too moist. And because the crust is usually still warm when filled, the prebaking hastens cooking time.

After extensive testing, we found two tricks to prebaking pie shells. First, the pie shell should be thoroughly chilled before baking, and second, aluminum foil, if pressed carefully into the cold shell, works well to prevent the crust from shrinking, eliminating the need for pie weights. (*See* figures 25 through 28.)

Master Recipe

American Pie Dough: Single Crust

➤ NOTE: *Make sure not to undercook your crusts; they should be nut brown, not light brown.*

8- or 9-Inch Pie Shell

1¼	cups all purpose flour
½	teaspoon salt
1	tablespoon sugar
6	tablespoons chilled unsalted butter
4	tablespoons chilled all-vegetable shortening
3–4	tablespoons ice water

10-Inch Regular or 9-Inch Deep-Dish Pie Shell

1½	cups all-purpose flour
½	teaspoon salt
1	tablespoon sugar
8	tablespoons chilled unsalted butter
4	tablespoons chilled all-vegetable shortening
4	tablespoons ice water

16

Master Instructions

➤ NOTE: *See pages 11–14 for a detailed description of the Master Instructions, and pages 22–39 for illustrations.*

1. Mix flour, salt, and sugar in food processor fitted with the steel blade. Cut butter into ¼-inch pieces.

2. Scatter butter pieces over flour mixture, tossing to coat butter with flour. Cut butter into flour with five 1-second pulses. Add shortening and continue cutting in until flour is pale yellow and resembles coarse cornmeal, with butter bits no larger than small peas, about four more 1-second pulses. Turn mixture into bowl.

3. Sprinkle 3 tablespoons of water over mixture. With rubber spatula, use folding motion to combine, then press down on dough until dough sticks together, adding up to 1 tablespoon more water if dough will not come together. Shape into ball with hands.

4. Flatten dough ball into 4-inch-wide disk. Dust lightly with flour, wrap in plastic, and refrigerate 30 minutes before rolling. Roll dough to 11-inch diameter (12-inch diameter for 10-inch or deep-dish shell) and finish shell referring to figures 13–21 (*see* pages 32–39).

Master Recipe

American Pie Dough: Double Crust

➤ **NOTE:** *Make sure not to undercook your crusts; they should be nut brown, not light brown.*

Double 8- or 9-Inch Pie Shell

2 ¼	cups all-purpose flour
1	teaspoon salt
2	tablespoons sugar
11	tablespoons chilled unsalted butter
7	tablespoons chilled all-vegetable shortening
4–5	tablespoons ice water

Double 10-Inch Regular or Double 9-Inch Deep-Dish Pie Shell

2 ½	cups all-purpose flour
1	teaspoon salt
2	tablespoons sugar
13	tablespoons chilled unsalted butter
8	tablespoons chilled all-vegetable shortening
5	tablespoons ice water

18

Master Instructions

➤ NOTE: *See pages 11–15 for a detailed description of the Master Instructions, and pages 22–41 for illustrations.*

1. Follow steps 1 through 3 (*see* page 17) for Single 8- or 9-Inch Pie Shell.

2. Divide dough into two balls, one slightly larger than the other, before shaping them into disks. Roll larger ball into an 11-inch round (12-inch diameter for 10-inch or deep-dish shell) and fit it into pie pan.

3. Push dough firmly into sides of pan, fill shell, and roll remaining dough into a 10-inch circle (11-inch circle for 10-inch or deep-dish shell) so that it will overhang the pan by about ½-inch all around.

4. Following figures 22–23 (*see* pages 40–41), place top dough round over filling, trim edges of both shells so they overhang the pan by ½-inch, press them together, and turn them under so that they are flush with the rim of the pan. Edge the pie shell following figures 19–21 (*see* pages 37–39).

Master Recipe

Single Prebaked Pie Crust

➤ NOTE: *Use a glass pie pan and the standard crust recipe, and you'll get terrific results. Usually, you'll want to start work on the filling as the crust bakes.*

8- or 9-Inch Pie Shell

1 recipe American Pie Dough for single-crust 8- or 9-inch shell (see page 16)

1 large egg yolk beaten with ⅛ teaspoon water

10-Inch Regular or 9-Inch Deep-Dish Pie Shell

1 recipe American Pie Dough for single-crust 10-inch regular or 9-inch deep-dish shell (see page 16)

1 large egg yolk beaten with ⅛ teaspoon water

Master Instructions

1. Follow steps 1 through 4 for single 8- or 9-inch pie shell in Master Recipe for American Pie Dough: Single Crust.

2. Refrigerate pie shell 20 minutes or freeze it 5 minutes. Prick bottom and sides of dough with fork at ½-inch intervals (*see* figure 25, page 42). Cut round of aluminum foil to cover inside shell completely, pressing it flush against corners, sides, and over rim. Prick all over once again (*see* figure 26, page 42). Chill at least 30 minutes longer, preferably 1 hour or more.

3. Adjust oven rack to lowest position and heat oven to 400 degrees. Bake shell 15 minutes, pressing down on foil with mitt-protected hands to flatten any puffs. Remove foil and bake 8 to 10 minutes longer, or until interior just begins to color.

4. Remove shell from oven, brush sides and bottom with egg yolk and return to oven until yolk glazes over, about 1 minute longer.

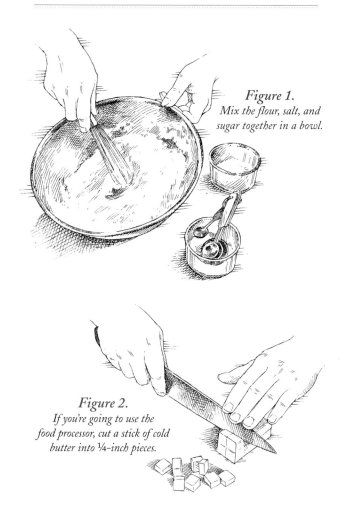

Figure 1.
Mix the flour, salt, and
sugar together in a bowl.

Figure 2.
If you're going to use the
food processor, cut a stick of cold
butter into 1/4-inch pieces.

Figure 3.
Correctly processed dough looks like coarse meal tossed with a
few pea-sized lumps. Be sure, however, that the flour is thoroughly
coated with shortening and takes on a slightly yellowish color.
It is better to overprocess this mixture than underprocess.

Figure 4.
If you prefer a pastry blender or your fingertips for mixing,
you can still use butter cubes, but many people find it easier to
grate a stick of cold butter directly into the flour.

Figure 5.
Using a pastry blender is easy: Just push it up and down
into the dough until you get the proper texture.

Figure 6.
To use your hands, rub the butter, flour, and shortening together
quickly, not allowing the fat to melt between your fingers.

Figure 7.
Sprinkle the mixture with ice water.

27

Figure 8.
Use a rubber spatula and a folding motion to mix in the water.
Press the dough into a ball with the spatula, adding additional
water only if necessary.

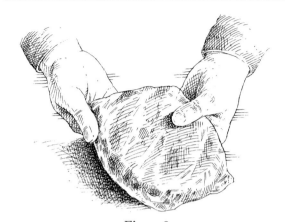

Figure 9.
Flatten the dough into a 4-inch-wide disk.

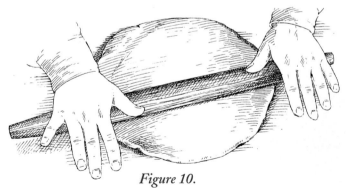

Figure 10.
To roll, apply light pressure to the dough with a flat rolling pin
and work from the center outwards.

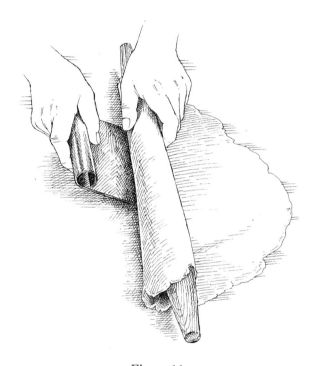

Figure 11.
About every thirty seconds, turn the dough over with a scraper
and rotate a quarter turn.

Figure 12.
To make sure that you've rolled the dough to the right size,
place the pie pan upside down on top of it; the diameter of the
dough should be 2 inches greater than that of the pie pan.

Figure 13.
Work your dough scraper under the dough, then roll the dough
onto a rolling pin to move it into the pie pan.

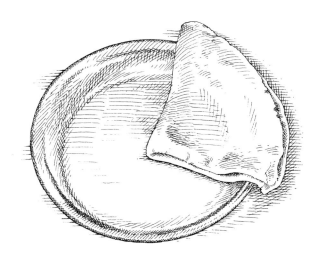

Figure 14.
Alternatively, fold the circle of dough in half,
and then in half again. Place the folded point of dough
in the center of the pan and unfold it gently.

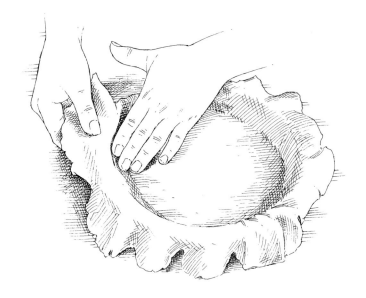

Figure 15.
For single-crust pies, push the dough firmly into the sides
of the pie pan to reduce shrinkage.

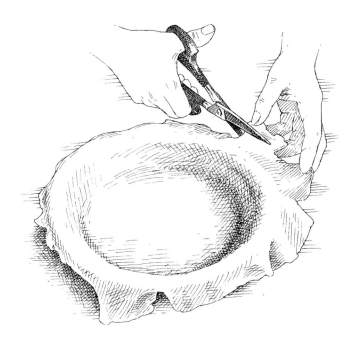

Figure 16.
Use scissors to trim the dough to ½ inch from the rim of the pan.

Figure 17.
Always save some of the trimming scraps.
Then, if a hole or tear develops in the shell, brush it with some
water and patch it with some of the reserved dough.

Figure 18.
When the crust is in place, fold the excess dough
under itself, pressing it firmly.

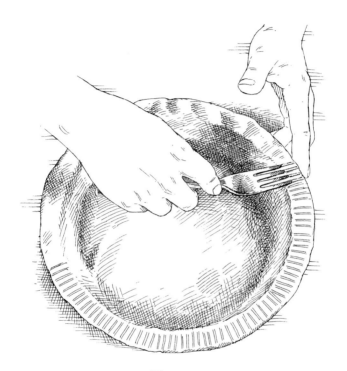

Figure 19.
The simplest decoration is made with a fork: Press it flat against
the shell's rim all around.

Figure 20.
You can make a more attractive rim by pressing with a finger into
the space created by the thumb and forefinger of the other hand.

Figure 21.
Or pinch the dough between your thumb and the side of your
forefinger to create a twisted-rope pattern.

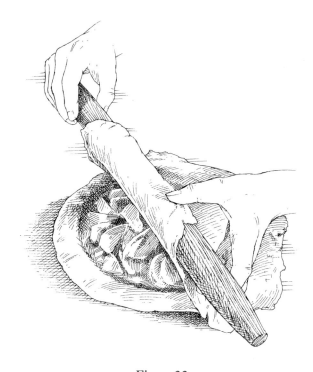

Figure 22.
For a double-crust pie, place the top shell onto the bottom, using
the technique from figure 13. Center it above the plate, then gently
unroll it over the filling onto the bottom shell.

Figure 23.
Trim the edges of both shells so that they overhang the pan
by about ½ inch. Press them together and turn them under so
that they are flush with the rim of the pan.

Figure 24.
Use a sharp knife to cut vents in the top shell.

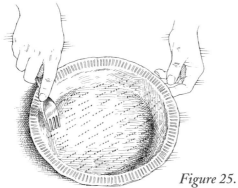

Figure 25.
Before prebaking a pie shell, prick it
all over with a fork at ½-inch intervals
to help reduce bubbling.

Figure 26.
Cover the inside of the shell completely with a round
of aluminum foil; prick once again with a fork.

42

Figure 27.
To prevent a filled prebaked crust
from overcooking, cut a round
out of a sheet of aluminum foil to
fit over the rim of the shell.

Figure 28.
Press foil onto rim, leaving top
of pie exposed.

chapter two

FRUIT PIES

ONCE YOU MASTER THE BASIC PIE crust, fruit pies become quite simple to make. Some, however, are simpler than others: Apple pie, for example, requires only apples, sugar, and a few spices.

For juicier fruits, however—such as stone fruits and berries—thickening becomes important. When a fruit pie is too liquid, the presentation is ruined. But the wrong thickener can ruin the flavor of a pie, so care must be taken.

There are, then, two goals in thickening the fruit in a pie: One is to preserve a little of the juice as liquid, binding the rest with the solids; the other is to avoid losing the clean, bright flavors of the fruit in the process. This is one of the great challenges of pie baking, and every thickener, from flour to cornstarch to ground nuts to arrowroot, has been used at one time or another.

We have tried them all and found that minute (quick-cooking) tapioca, which in itself is virtually tasteless, gives the best combination of clean flavor and good thickening power. (If you can find only pearl tapioca, just place it in a spice grinder, blender, or food processor and grind away for thirty seconds or so. Now you have minute tapioca.) The amount of tapioca to use varies, depending on the juiciness of the fruit and your personal taste (*see* Master Recipe for Fruit Pie, page 48, for details); we like some juice and therefore opt for the lower quantity recommended in the master recipe).

MAKING A LATTICE TOP

Making a lattice top for a fruit pie takes a couple of minutes longer than using a top shell, but it has a couple of distinct advantages: First of all, it lets more of the fruit flavor come through. And it also looks prettier. Follow the next four illustrations to learn how to make a lattice.

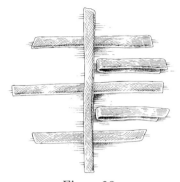

Figure 29.
Roll the dough in a circle as usual and cut it into ten strips, each
½-inch wide. Place five strips of dough across the top of the pie.
Fold the second and fourth strips in half and place a long strip of
dough down the center of the pie, at right angles to the other strips.

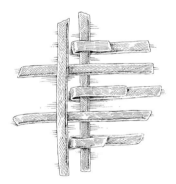

Figure 30.
Fold back the second and fourth strips and fold the other three strips
in half. Add a second strip of dough and fold back the folded strips.

46

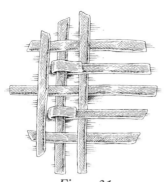

Figure 31.
Fold back the second and fourth strips for a second time and add a third strip of dough. Unfold the strips.

Figure 32.
Repeat this process on the other side of the pie, alternating folds and adding two more strips of dough (you will have a total of ten strips of dough, five running in each direction). Trim off the excess lattice ends, fold the rim of the shell up over the lattice strips, and crimp.

Master Recipe

Fruit Pie

➤ NOTE: *Take into account the sweetness of the fruit you're using to determine the correct amount of sugar. Tart berries need a full cup of sugar, but sweet ones are perfect with three-quarters of a cup, sometimes even a bit less. The amount of tapioca to use depends not only on the fruit but on your preference for juiciness in the sliced pie. If you want perfect individual pieces, with no juice running out onto the pie plate, use at least four tablespoons for juicy fruit, and three to four tablespoons for less-juicy fruit. Use less if you like some juices to flow. Allow at least an hour for the pie to set after you remove it from the oven, to allow the juices to thicken.*

1	recipe American Pie Dough for a double 8- or 9-inch pie shell (*see* page 18)
6	cups fruit, prepared (peeled, cored, sliced)
1	teaspoon grated orange or lemon zest
2	teaspoons fresh lemon juice
¾–1	cup sugar
3–4	tablespoons quick-cooking tapioca
2	tablespoons unsalted butter, cut into small pieces (optional)

48

Master Instructions

1. While dough is chilling, heat oven to 400 degrees.

2. Toss fruit with other ingredients except butter and let sit 15 minutes.

3. Roll larger ball of dough, fit it into pie pan, and trim it (for a lattice top, leave ½-inch of dough all around). Add fruit mixture and dot with butter if you like.

4. Place bottom crust in freezer while you roll out top crust. Lay this over the pie and trim, leaving ½-inch of overlap. Fold top layer under bottom layer and finish crust edge. Or create a lattice top (*see* figures 29–32, page 46–47).

5. Use sharp knife to cut air vents. If dough is very soft, place in freezer 10 minutes before baking.

6. Place pie on baking sheet in oven; turn oven down to 350 degrees. Check after 35 minutes and rotate if pie is not browning evenly. Bake 1 hour; pie crust should be nut brown in color and juices should bubble before you remove pie from oven.

7. Let pie sit at least 1 hour to allow juices to thicken.

Apple Pie

➤ NOTE: *The proper variety of apple is everything to a good apple pie. We tested every variety we could lay our hands on. The best are Golden Delicious, Baldwin, Macoun, Northern Spy, and Ida Red. The worst are Rome Beauty, Red Delicious, McIntosh, and Granny Smith. Before you cook with any apple, bite into it. If it has firm texture, bright flavor with a hint of a bite, and a good amount of juice, it will probably bake nicely in a pie.*

1	recipe American Pie Dough for double 8- or 9-inch pie shell (*see* page 18)
6	cups apples, peeled, cored, and sliced
1	teaspoon grated orange or lemon zest
2	teaspoons fresh lemon juice
¼	teaspoon salt
½	teaspoon ground cinnamon
¼	teaspoon ground allspice
⅛	teaspoon freshly grated nutmeg
¾	cup sugar
4	tablespoons unsalted butter, cut into small pieces (optional)

⁜ INSTRUCTIONS: Follow Master Recipe instructions for Fruit Pie (*see* page 49). Add 1 tablespoon quick-cooking tapioca if apples are very juicy.

Figure 33.
Peel the apple and core it. Cut a thin slice from one end so that
the apple sits squarely on your cutting surface. This makes it easy
to cut thin, uniform slices. Now divide the apple in half
vertically and cut off individual slices.

Figure 34.
If you cover your grater with waxed paper before grating
lemon zest, the zest will remain on top of the waxed paper rather
than clogging the grater's holes.

Peach Pie

➤ N O T E : *Peaches must be peeled for pie, but the method is easy. Bring a large pot of water to a boil. Place the peaches in the water, a few at a time, for just thirty seconds. (If your peaches are not ripe, boil them for forty-five seconds.) Remove them with a slotted spoon and immediately immerse in ice water. When they cool, peel with a paring knife.*

1	recipe American Pie Dough for double 8- or 9-inch pie shell (*see* page 18)
6	cups peaches, peeled, pitted, and sliced
1	teaspoon grated orange or lemon zest
2	teaspoons fresh lemon juice
½	cup brown sugar
¼–½	cup granulated sugar, depending on the ripeness of the peaches
1	tablespoon crystallized ginger, minced (optional)
¼	teaspoon freshly grated nutmeg
¼	teaspoon ground allspice
¼	teaspoon salt
3–4	tablespoons quick-cooking tapioca
2	tablespoons unsalted butter, cut into small pieces (optional)

▚ I N S T R U C T I O N S : Follow Master Recipe instructions for Fruit Pie (*see* page 49).

Strawberry-Rhubarb Pie

1	recipe American Pie Dough for double 8- or 9-inch pie shell (*see* page 18)
3	cups strawberries, hulled and sliced
3	cups rhubarb, strung and cut into 1-inch pieces
1	tablespoon grated orange or lemon zest
2	teaspoons fresh lemon juice
¼	teaspoon vanilla extract
¾–1	cup sugar
3–4	tablespoons quick-cooking tapioca
2	tablespoons unsalted butter, cut into small pieces (optional)

INSTRUCTIONS: Follow Master Recipe instructions for Fruit Pie (*see* page 49).

Blueberry Pie

➤ NOTE: *This same recipe can be used with blackberries or raspberries.*

1	recipe American Pie Dough for double 8- or 9-inch pie shell (*see* page 18)
6	cups blueberries, picked over
¼	teaspoon ground allspice
	Pinch freshly grated nutmeg
2	teaspoons fresh lemon juice plus 1 teaspoon zest from 1 lemon
¾ –1	cup sugar
3–4	tablespoons quick-cooking tapioca
2	tablespoons unsalted butter, cut into small pieces (optional)

INSTRUCTIONS: Follow Master Recipe instructions for Fruit Pie (*see* page 49).

Cherry Pie

➤ NOTE: *If you can only find cherries that have been canned in syrup, drain and rinse them with water, then drain them again before proceding.*

1	recipe American Pie Dough for double 8- or 9-inch pie shell (*see* page 18)
6	cups pitted, canned sour cherries packed in water
2	teaspoons fresh lemon juice
$\frac{1}{8}$	teaspoon ground allspice
$\frac{1}{8}$	teaspoon ground cinnamon
$\frac{1}{8}$	teaspoon almond extract
1	tablespoon brandy
1	cup sugar
$\frac{1}{4}$	cup quick-cooking tapioca
2	tablespoons unsalted butter, cut into small pieces (optional)

INSTRUCTIONS: Follow Master Recipe instructions for Fruit Pie (*see* page 49).

chapter three

CUSTARD PIES

ITH THE PERFECT COMBINATION OF ingredients, anyone can produce a light, delicate, and delicious custard for a pie. We've tried just about every possible combination of eggs, sugar, milk, and cream (as well as a few nontraditional ingredients). For example, we varied the proportion of cream to milk, trying all milk (which not only lacked flavor but produced a pie that collapsed in the middle during baking) and two parts cream to one part milk (which yielded a heavy texture with a filmy aftertaste).

Finally, we settled on the proportions you'll find in the master recipe. You need heavy cream and whole eggs (skim milk and egg whites don't cut it), plus lots of sugar to make a good custard. All add incomparable flavor, reduce the likelihood of curdling, and make a truly silky pie.

But even with the proper ingredients, there is a further challenge in making custard pie: baking. If you bake our pie at 350 degrees, the custard will toughen by the time the pie sets. (It may remind you of an overcooked custard pie at a third-rate diner.) Although most custards require gentle treatment, you need a hot oven—400 degrees—for a custard pie. Because it sets the filling quickly, high oven heat works to the advantage of all custard pies.

But baking at high heat also has its perils: Custard will curdle and become grainy and watery when overbaked. How do you prevent this? You must be brave and immediately take the pie out of the oven once the center no longer sloshes but only wiggles like gelatin when the pan is gently shaken. Residual heat will finish the cooking outside the oven.

With four cups of liquid in the crust, creating a crisp pastry becomes a problem. We have the solution: First, begin by baking the crust almost completely before filling it. Then, make sure that both crust and filling are hot when you assemble the pie so the custard can begin firming up immediately, before it soaks into the pastry. Finally, bake the pie quickly, in the bottom of the oven, where the bottom of the crust is exposed to the most intense heat.

Master Recipe

Custard Pie

➤ NOTE: *Start making the filling after you begin pre-baking the crust. When baking the custard, be sure to remove the pie from the oven when the middle two inches is still quite wobbly; the custard will continue cooking once it is removed from the oven.*

1	hot prebaked single-crust 8- or 9-inch pie crust (*see* page 20)
2	cups milk
1	cup heavy cream
4	large eggs
⅔	cup sugar
1	teaspoon vanilla extract
½	teaspoon freshly grated nutmeg
¼	teaspoon salt

Master Instructions

1. Heat oven to 400 degrees. Heat milk and heavy cream over medium-low heat in saucepan until mixture starts to steam. Pour into 4-cup glass measuring cup and let cool. Gently whisk together eggs, sugar, vanilla, nutmeg, and salt. Pour the milk-cream mixture into the egg mixture, whisking gently.

2. Place hot pie crust on baking sheet on lowest rack of oven. With rack pulled halfway out, pour in custard mixture. Close oven door and bake 25 to 30 minutes.

3. Remove pie from oven when perimeter is set but middle two inches is still wobbly. Cool on wire rack at least 2 hours before serving.

Orange Custard Pie

➤ NOTE: *The addition of orange juice loosens the custard a bit, so we've added an extra egg yolk to make sure it sets up properly.*

1   hot prebaked single-crust 8- or 9-inch
    pie crust (*see* page 20)

4   large eggs
1   egg yolk
1   tablespoon minced (not grated) orange zest
¼   cup orange juice
¾   cup sugar
½   teaspoon vanilla extract
¼   teaspoon salt
2   cups milk
1   cup heavy cream

■ INSTRUCTIONS: Follow Master Recipe instructions for Custard Pie (*see* page 59), whisking orange zest and juice into the egg mixture.

60

Coconut Custard Pie

➤ NOTE: *Look in your local health foods store for unsweetened dried coconut.*

1	hot prebaked single-crust 8- or 9-inch pie crust (*see* page 20)
3	large eggs
$\frac{2}{3}$	cup sugar
$\frac{3}{4}$	teaspoon vanilla extract
$\frac{1}{2}$	teaspoon freshly grated nutmeg
$\frac{1}{4}$	teaspoon salt
$1\frac{1}{2}$	cups milk
$\frac{3}{4}$	cup heavy cream
1	cup shredded dried coconut

INSTRUCTIONS: Follow Master Recipe instructions for Custard Pie (*see* page 59), adding coconut along with milk and cream. If you like, toast the coconut first by cooking it over medium-low heat in dry skillet, stirring almost constantly, until lightly browned.

61

chapter four

CREAM PIES

REAM PIE HAS ALMOST UNIVERSAL APPEAL, with enough flavors to satisfy anyone. Here, the trick is to create a filling that is soft and creamy, yet stiff enough to cut cleanly. It's not as easy as it sounds.

In our tests, adding flour left us with a filling that was too soft; gelatin became rubbery. Tapioca, which worked so well with fruit, produced a filling with the texture of stewed okra. And so on. Only cornstarch coupled with egg yolks gave us the results we sought (whole eggs yielded a grainy texture). The other ingredients are more or less standard although the milk component proved tricky: Cream is simply too rich for a pie that already contains butter and eggs. Skim milk tastes thin and lacks the creamy texture we all love. Both 2 percent and whole milk work well, but they work even better when combined with a bit of evaporated milk, which adds a rich, round, caramel flavor. The basic vanilla cream filling also benefits greatly from using vanilla beans in place of extract.

When making a cream filling for a pie, some cooks heat the sugar, cornstarch, and milk to a simmer, gradually add some of this mixture to the yolks to stabilize them, and then return the stabilized yolks to the rest of the simmering milk. But you can also dump everything except the flavorings and butter into a saucepan and cook, stirring fairly constantly, until the mixture begins to bubble. It's simpler, and because the cornstarch prevents the eggs from curdling, it isn't that risky.

Developing a filling with great body and flavor is key, but preventing that filling from turning the crust soggy is almost as important. Unlike custard pie, in which the filling bakes in the crust, cream pie unites a fully cooked crust with a moist, fluid filling. We found two procedures that help to keep the crust crisp. The first is to coat the pastry lightly with graham cracker crumbs when rolling it out; this helps it retain its light, crisp texture when the filling is added.

It also helps to pour filling into its crust while the filling is warm but not quite hot. Cooled filling makes the crust soggy. Hot filling keeps it crisp, but because it is still quite liquid when poured into the crust, it settles compactly and falls apart when sliced. Just-warm filling, having had a chance to set a bit, mounds when poured into the crust and slices beautifully; it's the best option.

Finally, there is the topping of the pie. Properly whipped cream requires no special tricks to hold up on the pie, even overnight. The type of sugar you use doesn't matter much, although if you're serving the pie immediately, it helps to use confectioners' sugar rather than granulated sugar, which takes a little while to dissolve. The most important choice you can make in whipped cream is the cream itself. If you can, always go for pasteurized (or even raw) cream and avoid ultrapasteurized cream, which has a distinctly cooked flavor.

Figure 35.
For extra crispness, roll the crust in graham cracker crumbs
before baking.

Graham Cracker–Coated Pie Crust for Cream Pies

➤ NOTE: *This easy adaptation of the basic pie crust guarantees crispness. We use it for Lemon Meringue Pie as well.*

1	recipe American Pie Dough for single-crust 8- or 9-inch pie (*see* page 16)
½	cup graham cracker crumbs

INSTRUCTIONS:

1. Follow Master Recipe for American Pie Dough through point where you remove disk from refrigerator.

2. Sprinkle work area with 2 tablespoons graham cracker crumbs. Remove dough from wrapping and place in center of work area. Scatter a few more crumbs over top (*see* figure 35). Roll dough in accordance with master recipe, rotating a quarter turn after each stroke and sprinkling additional crumbs underneath and on top, as necessary, to coat dough heavily. Flip dough and continue to roll it until about 13 inches in diameter and just under ⅛-inch thick.

3. Place dough in center of 9-inch pie pan. Trim crust and finish it with design in accordance with master recipe.

Vanilla Cream Pie

➤ NOTE: *You can start putting this together as soon as the crust goes into the oven; both filling and crust will reach the correct temperatures before you combine them. Leftover pie can be refrigerated and eaten the next day.*

| 1 | Graham Cracker–Coated Pie Crust, baked and cooled completely (*see* page 66) |

Vanilla Cream Filling

10	tablespoons granulated sugar
¼	cup cornstarch
⅛	teaspoon salt
5	large egg yolks, lightly beaten
2	cups milk
½	cup evaporated milk
½	vanilla bean, 3 inches long and split lengthwise
2	tablespoons unsalted butter
1	teaspoon brandy

Whipped Cream Topping

1	cup heavy cream, preferably not ultrapasteurized
2	tablespoons confectioners' sugar
½	teaspoon vanilla extract

⁝⁝ INSTRUCTIONS: Vanilla Cream Pie

1. *For the filling:* Whisk granulated sugar, cornstarch, and salt together in medium saucepan. Add yolks. Immediately but gradually whisk in milks. Drop in vanilla bean.

2. Cook over medium heat, stirring, until mixture starts to thicken and begins to simmer, 8 to 12 minutes. Once mixture begins to simmer, continue to cook, stirring constantly, 1 minute longer. Remove vanilla bean, scrape out seeds (*see* figures 36 and 37), and whisk them back into pudding along with butter and brandy.

3. Pour filling into shallow pan (another pie pan works well). Put plastic wrap directly over filling surface to prevent skin from forming; cool just until warm, about 30 minutes. (If filling cools for too long before transfer, it could turn soupy.)

4. Pour warm filling into crust and, once again, place sheet of plastic wrap over filling surface. Refrigerate until completely chilled, at least 3 hours.

5. *For the topping:* Whip cream to soft peaks. Add confectioners' sugar and vanilla; continue to whip to barely stiff peaks. Spread over filling and refrigerate until ready to serve.

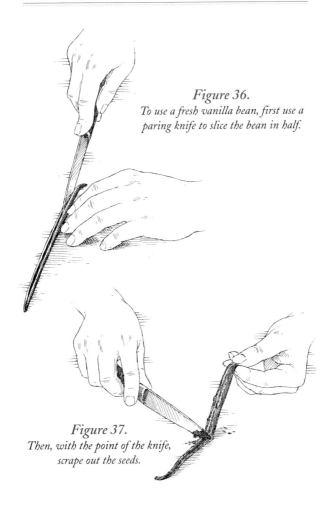

Figure 36.
To use a fresh vanilla bean, first use a
paring knife to slice the bean in half.

Figure 37.
Then, with the point of the knife,
scrape out the seeds.

Chocolate Cream Pie

➤ NOTE: *Cocoa alone is mild and pleasant; semi- or bittersweet chocolate offers an intense hit but dies on the tongue. The best chocolate cream pie needs a little of each—bittersweet for intensity, cocoa for lingering chocolate flavor.*

1	Graham Cracker–Coated Pie Crust, baked and cooled completely (*see* page 66)

Chocolate Cream Filling

10	tablespoons granulated sugar
2	tablespoons unsweetened cocoa
¼	cup cornstarch
⅛	teaspoon salt
5	large egg yolks, lightly beaten
2	cups milk
½	cup evaporated milk
1	teaspoon vanilla extract
2	tablespoons unsalted butter
4	ounces semi- or bittersweet chocolate, shaved (*see* figure 38)
1	teaspoon brandy

70

Whipped Cream Topping

1 cup heavy cream, preferably not ultrapasteurized

2 tablespoons confectioners' sugar

½ teaspoon vanilla extract

⁘ INSTRUCTIONS: Follow recipe instructions for Vanilla Cream Pie (*see* page 68), adding cocoa to cornstarch mixture and chocolate along with butter and brandy. Substitute vanilla extract for vanilla bean.

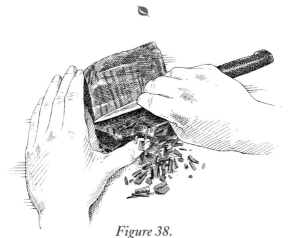

Figure 38.
To shave chocolate, scrape the top of a bar, towards you, with a paring knife.

71

Coconut Cream Pie

➤ **NOTE:** *Unsweetened coconut (from a health foods store) or sweetened flaked coconut from the supermarket both work fine here. Either needs to be toasted first: Untoasted coconut offers little more than texture, while toasted coconut brings the pie to life. To toast it, cook the coconut over medium-low heat in a dry skillet, stirring almost constantly, until the flakes are lightly browned. Cool the coconut to room temperature.*

1	Graham Cracker–Coated Pie Crust, baked and cooled completely (*see* page 66)

Coconut Cream Filling

1¼	cups flaked sweetened or unsweetened coconut
10	tablespoons granulated sugar
¼	cup cornstarch
⅛	teaspoon salt
5	large egg yolks, lightly beaten
2	cups milk
½	cup evaporated milk
½	vanilla bean, 3 inches long and split lengthwise
2	tablespoons unsalted butter
1	teaspoon brandy

Whipped Cream Topping

1 cup heavy cream, preferably not
ultrapasteurized

2 tablespoons confectioners' sugar

½ teaspoon vanilla extract

INSTRUCTIONS: Follow recipe instructions for Vanilla Cream Pie (*see* page 68), stirring 1 cup of the coconut into filling once butter has melted. Continue with recipe, sprinkling the remaining toasted coconut over whipped cream topping.

Banana Cream Pie

➤ **NOTE:** *The best place for the banana slices is in the middle of the filling. If you slice them directly over the pie crust, they'll moisten it. If you slice them over the filling top, they'll quickly turn brown.*

1	Graham Cracker–Coated Pie Crust, baked and cooled completely (*see* page 66)

Banana Cream Filling

10	tablespoons granulated sugar
¼	cup cornstarch
⅛	teaspoon salt
5	large egg yolks, lightly beaten
2	cups milk
½	cup evaporated milk
½	vanilla bean, 3 inches long and split lengthwise
2	tablespoons unsalted butter
1	teaspoon brandy
2	medium bananas

Whipped Cream Topping

1	cup heavy cream, preferably not ultrapasteurized
2	tablespoons confectioners' sugar
½	teaspoon vanilla extract

INSTRUCTIONS: Follow recipe instructions for Vanilla Cream Pie (*see* page 68). Spoon half the warm filling into baked and cooled pie crust. Top with bananas, then pile in remaining filling. Continue with recipe.

75

Butterscotch Cream Pie

➤ NOTE: *Although caramelizing the sugar makes this pie a bit more work than the others, it's worth the effort.*

1 Graham Cracker–Coated Pie Crust, baked and cooled completely (*see* page 66)

Butterscotch Cream Filling

¼ cup cornstarch

¼ teaspoon salt

½ cup evaporated milk

5 large egg yolks

6 tablespoons unsalted butter

1 cup light brown sugar

2 cups whole milk

1 teaspoon vanilla extract

Whipped Cream Topping

1 cup heavy cream, preferably not ultrapasteurized

2 tablespoons confectioners' sugar

½ teaspoon vanilla extract

INSTRUCTIONS:

1. Dissolve cornstarch and salt in evaporated milk; whisk in egg yolks and set aside.

2. Heat butter and sugar in medium saucepan over medium heat until candy thermometer registers 220 degrees, about 5 minutes. Gradually whisk in whole milk. When sugar dissolves, gradually whisk in cornstarch mixture. Continue cooking, stirring frequently, until mixture comes to a boil, 2 or 3 minutes, then cook 1 minute longer, stirring.

3. Turn off heat and stir in vanilla. Pour filling into shallow pan (a pie pan works well) and finish as in recipe for Vanilla Cream Pie (*see* page 68).

77

chapter five

LEMON MERINGUE PIE

HE IDEAL LEMON MERINGUE PIE HAS a rich filling that balances the airy meringue without detracting from the flavor of lemon. Like a cream pie filling, the meringue filling should be soft but not runny, firm enough to cut but not stiff and gelatinous. Finally, the meringue itself should not break down and puddle on the bottom or "weep" on top—not even on rainy days.

The ingredients in lemon meringue pie have remained constant for more than a century: sugar, water (or sometimes milk), cornstarch (sometimes part flour), egg yolks, lemon juice (and usually zest), and a little butter. The straightforward lemon flavor of the water-based filling is pleasant, but it is also one-dimensional, lacking depth. Milk, however, subdues the lemon flavor. The solution is to rely primarily on water and egg yolks, eliminating the milk altogether. This has another benefit: The addition of egg yolks allows you to cut back on both sugar (which acts as a softener at a certain level) and cornstarch, and still achieve a firm yet tender filling.

MERINGUE

Finally, there is the meringue. On any given day, meringue may shrink, bead, puddle, deflate, burn, sweat, break down, or turn rubbery. The pudding underneath the meringue can come from undercooking the whites, which break down and return to their liquid state. The beading (or weeping) on top of the pie results from overcooking, causing proteins in the egg white to coagulate and squeeze out moisture, which surfaces as tears or beads. Although this double dilemma may seem insurmountable, it is not. If the filling is piping hot, the meringue will not undercook; if the oven temperature is relatively low, it will not overcook. And a relatively low oven temperature produces the best-looking, most evenly browned meringues. To further stabilize the meringue, we like to beat in a tiny bit of cornstarch; if you do this, your meringue will not weep, even on hot, humid days.

Lemon Meringue Pie

➤ NOTE: *Like cream pies, lemon meringue pie has fully cooked filling added to an already-cooked crust. So once again we've turned to the graham cracker crumb–augmented pie dough to ensure crispness. The graham cracker crumbs add a wonderful flavor that complements the lemon pie without masking the character of the dough itself.*

1	Graham Cracker–Coated Pie Crust, baked and cooled completely (*see* page 66)

Lemon Filling

1	cup sugar
¼	cup cornstarch
⅛	teaspoon salt
6	large egg yolks
1	tablespoon zest from 1 lemon (*see* figure 34)
½	cup juice from 2 or 3 lemons
2	tablespoons unsalted butter

Meringue Topping

1	tablespoon cornstarch
¼	teaspoon cream of tartar
½	cup sugar
4	large egg whites
½	teaspoon vanilla extract

80

Figure 39.
Put dabs of meringue over the lemon filling:
It makes it easier to spread.

:: INSTRUCTIONS: Lemon Meringue Pie

1. *For the filling:* Mix first three filling ingredients and 1½ cups cold water in large, nonreactive saucepan. Bring mixture to simmer over medium heat, whisking occasionally at beginning of process and more frequently as mixture begins to thicken. When mixture starts to simmer and turn translucent, whisk in egg yolks, two at a time. Whisk in zest, then lemon juice, and finally butter.

2. Bring mixture back to simmer, whisking constantly. Remove from heat and place layer of plastic wrap directly on surface of filling to keep it hot and prevent skin from forming.

3. *For the topping:* Mix cornstarch with ⅓ cup water in small saucepan. Bring to simmer, whisking occasionally at the beginning and more frequently as mixture thickens. When mixture starts to simmer and turn translucent, remove from heat. Let cool.

4. Heat oven to 325 degrees. Mix cream of tartar and sugar together. Beat egg whites and vanilla until frothy. Beat in sugar mixture, 1 tablespoon at a time, until sugar is fully incorporated and mixture forms soft peaks. Add cornstarch mixture, 1 tablespoon at a time; continue to beat until meringue stands in stiff peaks. During last minute or so of beating meringue, remove plastic and return filling to low heat.

5. Pour filling into pie crust. Use rubber spatula to distribute meringue evenly around edge, then center of pie (*see* figure 39). Make sure meringue attaches to crust to prevent shrinking (*see* figure 40).

6. Use spoon to create peaks all over meringue. Bake until meringue is golden brown, about 20 minutes. Transfer to wire rack and cool to room temperature before serving.

Figure 40.
Make sure to "anchor" the meringue to the edge of the crust or it may pull away and shrink.

83

chapter six

PUMPKIN PIE

HE COLONIAL FORERUNNERS OF PUMPKIN pie, called "puddings," were essentially rich custards in pastry with a bit of pumpkin and spice added. Today, the best pumpkin pies remain little more than variations on custard pie and present the baker with the same challenge: making the crust crisp while developing a custard that is firm yet still tender. But pumpkin pie is closer to foolproof than its pure custard cousins. This is because the pumpkin dilutes the egg proteins and interferes with curdling, giving you a longer window between "set" and "curdled."

Colonial bakers, of course, started with fresh pumpkin,

which they stewed, strained, and pressed dry between heavy cloth napkins. However, canned pumpkin takes very little work to make it behave beautifully. Its fibrous nature is easily corrected by pureeing it in a food processor or blender. And you can freshen its canned taste by cooking it with the sugar and spices before combining it with the custard ingredients. As the pumpkin simmers, its aroma becomes better and better, a small but delightful culinary miracle.

If you do not have a food processor, put the pumpkin through a food mill. Alternatively, you can cook the pumpkin, sugar, and spices together, then whir the mixture in a blender, adding enough of the cream called for in the recipe to permit the pumpkin to flow easily over the blades. In either case, heat the pumpkin with the (remaining) cream and milk, as indicated in the recipe, then slowly whisk the mixture into the beaten eggs.

For the sake of convenience, start making the filling for this pie as soon as you put the shell in the oven. If, after filling the crust and returning the pie to the oven, the rim of the shell appears to be browning too rapidly, cut a round of aluminum foil (*see* figures 27 and 28, page 43) and press it onto the rim. (Even easier is to cut the rim from a disposable pie plate and use that as a shield.) When the crust is done, cool it on a wire rack at least 1 hour. This pie is best at room temperature, but you can serve it slightly warm or chilled.

Pumpkin Pie

1 hot prebaked single-crust 8- or 9-inch pie crust (*see* page 20)

Pumpkin Filling

2 cups (16 ounces) plain pumpkin puree, canned or fresh

1 cup dark brown sugar

2 teaspoons ground ginger

2 teaspoons ground cinnamon

1 teaspoon freshly grated nutmeg

¼ teaspoon ground cloves

½ teaspoon salt

⅔ cup heavy cream

⅔ cup milk

4 large eggs

Whipped Cream Topping

1⅓ cups heavy cream, cold

3 tablespoons confectioners' sugar

1 tablespoon brandy

▪▪ REMINDER: If the rim of the shell is browning too rapidly, protect it with foil (*see* figures 27 and 28, page 43).

INSTRUCTIONS:

1. *For the filling:* Process pumpkin, brown sugar, ginger, cinnamon, nutmeg, cloves, and salt in food processor fitted with the steel blade for 1 minute.

2. Transfer mixture to 3-quart heavy-bottomed saucepan; bring to sputtering simmer over medium-high heat. Cook, stirring constantly, until thick and shiny, about 5 minutes.

3. As soon as pie crust comes out of oven, whisk cream and milk into pumpkin and bring to bare simmer. Process eggs in food processor until whites and yolks are mixed, about 5 seconds. With motor running, slowly pour about half of hot pumpkin mixture through feed tube. Stop machine and scrape in remaining pumpkin. Process 30 seconds longer.

4. Immediately pour warm filling into hot crust. (Ladle any excess filling into pie after it has baked 5 minutes or so; by this time filling will have settled.) Bake until filling is puffed, dry-looking, and lightly cracked around edges, and its center wiggles like gelatin when pie is gently shaken, about 25 minutes.

5. *For the topping:* Beat cream at medium speed to soft peaks; gradually add confectioners' sugar, then brandy. Beat to stiff peaks. Serve each wedge with dollop of whipped cream.

chapter seven

PECAN PIES

ECAN PIE IS YET ANOTHER CUSTARD, BUT a special one, containing butter and no cream. Because of its unique color and texture, gauging the right moment at which to take a pecan pie out of the oven remains difficult. Most cooks find that the occurrences of overcooked edges or undercooked middle are more frequent than with other pies.

The key lies, once again, in a hot prebaked crust. But you also need the correct oven temperature and a great deal of faith. Difficult as it may be to believe, you can only get a soft, smooth, creamy pecan pie by removing it from the oven when the center is still only the texture of gelatin. The pie will continue to cook as heat travels from the edges to the middle by conduction. And because pecan pies contain such a high percentage of sugar and butter, cooling makes them still more solid.

Finding the right oven temperature took us a while. Hot ovens of 375 degrees and over caused pie edges to solidify long before the centers thickened. Moderate ovens were better, but still resulted in curdled edges. A very slow oven—just 275 degrees—turned out to be best, consistently yielding pies with nicely thickened centers but without hardened rims.

Even after we determined this, however, a problem remained. Pies baked this slowly take so long to firm up that the crusts turn soggy, even when they are thoroughly prebaked and glazed with egg yolk. The solution is the same as it is for Lemon Meringue Pie: Heat the filling first. This cuts the baking time in half and keeps the crust crisp.

A word about the pecans: Pretoasting makes a big difference. The easiest way to do this is to pop them in the oven while it's preheating for the crust. They take only about seven minutes, but watch them carefully and stir them up from time to time to prevent them from burning. Finally, be sure to let the nuts cool to lukewarm before chopping them, or they will crumble. Also, use a knife; the food processor cuts the nuts too fine. With chopped, instead of whole nuts, the pie is easily sliced.

Master Recipe

Pecan Pie

➤ NOTE: *If you want warm pie, first cool it before cutting, then warm it in a 250-degree oven for about twenty minutes.*

1	hot prebaked single-crust 8- or 9-inch pie crust (*see* page 20)
6	tablespoons unsalted butter, cut into 1-inch pieces
1	cup dark brown sugar
½	teaspoon salt
3	large eggs
¾	cup light corn syrup
1	tablespoon vanilla extract
2	cups pecans (8 ounces)

▪▪ REMINDER: If the rim of the shell is browning too rapidly, protect it with aluminum foil (*see* figures 27 and 28, page 43).